TIO ZUCO

CONTENTS

The Chronicles of
TIO ZUCO

Weird Tales of Crime and Humor

by

Richard Trujillo

The Chronicles of Tio Zuco: Weird Tales of Crime and Humor
© Copyright 2005 Richard Trujillo. All Rights Reserved.

Author: Richard Trujillo
Introduction by Vicente M. Martinez
Editor: Bill Whaley
Copy Editing / Proofing by Helen Rynaski and Steve Fox
Graphic Design: WinkVisual Arts

FIRST EDITION 2017

ISBN: 978-0-9973950-1-3

Author's Note

I WOULD LIKE TO DEDICATE my book to my friend Bill Whaley who has helped me make it through the rain more than once and who—as my agent—when they give me the electric pew for shooting a priest, gets ten percent of the current.

I would also like to thank my friend David Griggs for helping me put the book together and who said, "Get this shit out of here and don't bring it back until it has more crime and sex in it."

Also my friend David Winter who said after reading the book, "What! This is outrageous. I'm not even mentioned in here. What about the time I held your carbine while you did the nasty with that bitch behind the bushes—doesn't that count? Or that time I drove the getaway car with you in the trunk when the fat boys were hunting your ass? Oh! How soon they forget. I want my money back." Too late, I had already spent it on drugs, pussy and Rock & Roll—all 20 dollars of it.

As for the rest of you, may I just say that I sincerely hope and pray that you get everything that you've got coming to you.

P.S.

Before any religious fanatics get their panties in an uproar, remember that "priest" could mean voodoo, Mayan, Egyptian or even the priest who blesses your white alabaster nalgas under the light of the silvery moon.

Yours in the Everlasting Faith

while still strumming and humming

the "Vato Loco Blues."

Your Cynical Friend,

Richard

Tio Zuco

A.K.A. Richard Trujillo

PHOTO BY DAVID GRIGGS

Contents

    Author's Note v
    Introduction x
1. Nine Ball Tommy 1
2. From a Barred Window Revisited 3
3. Shooting at and Getting Shot by Friend or Foe 4
4. The Last Run of a Diehard Chuco 6
5. Snake and Gun Story 8
6. Blues for a Night Screen Dancer 10
7. Ode to a Hollow Hawk 12
8. Dora the Cat's Walloping Wizards
    Magic Wand Contest 14
9. All the Broken Glass (Adventures From
    My Bar and Other Fun Games) 18
10. The Girl Who Climbed Me
    (Or the Conquering of Mt. Zuco) 20
11. Of Cops, Corruption and Sweet Revenge 22
12. Ronnie the Rat's Innovative Dance Gig 25
13. Tio Zuco's 24-hr. Barred Window
    Joint Sales and Emporium 27
14. Ballad of the Golden Spike
    and the Atomic Hurl 30
15. The Rocky Roads of General Hogwash
    (Low Lifes in My Life) 33
16. A Prayer for Harmony Raine
    (Santa on the Rocks) 36
17. Humito's Strange Revenge ....
    (Feathered Friend Blues) 38
18. The Gateways of Oblivion
    (It's Been a Good Run!) 40
19. Parable:God and the Devil Fighting over Me
    (Quarrel) 41

Introduction

By Vicente M. Martinez

I FIRST MET RICHARD in the late 1950s when I was in high school in Taos. He was dating the sister of a friend and I used to see him at their house. While he always acknowledged my presence with an "orale!" Richard kept to himself. Even then his presence commanded respect with a modicum of fear. It was not until the late 60s and 70s that I finally got to know him better while we were hanging out in the bars around Taos. Then, as now, he was a very gifted storyteller and humorist. At Tano's, and in other bars, he was able to keep everyone engaged and rolling in laughter with stories based on his own life experience. Not many doubted the authenticity of the stories, and skeptics had to bite their tongues lest they face his not-so-humorous glare.

In 1999 Richard self-published *The Barbarian Dialects,* his collection of dark-humored poetry, or as John Nichols stated, "a combination of poetry, blues, sci-fi, metal mustic, or just a simple cry from the dark." He soon earned his literary chops from a cross-section of of the Taos community bar flies, hippies, stoners, his literary and not-so-literary peers, intellectuals, artists, and tourists. Within a matter of time he began participating in poetry readings around town with much acclaim.

Now with the self-pulbication of short stories in *Chronicles of Tio Zuco: Weird Tales of Crime and Humor,* he creates vivid memories of the people and places of which he writes: Tommy's Pool Hall across from Cantu's, whacky Taos cops, the jail in the old courthouse on the Plaza with windows facing the back alley, where visiting hours were 24/7; the implicit danger of drugs in the Upper Rio Grande Valley, and runs to El Paso/Juarez on the historic Camino Real. Only the names of the characters have been changed to protect the not-so-innocent. Infused with sex, drugs, rock and roll, his tales will keep the reader engaged, amazed, and laughing.

Storytelling is an oral tradition and a vital part of the cultural fabric of the Chicano/Hispano communities of New Mexico. Transmitted from generation to generation, storytelling is a way of transmitting culture, history, knowledge, and values in order keep the community alive and vibrant. In his writing, he uses a combination of the *cuento* (story) and *chiste* (joke) to weave his personal experiences into serious and humorous vignettes.

Richard, who dropped out of school in the 10th grade but got a "higher" education in the state pen, is the last of a dying breed: *el chuco, el vato loco*, and is now a *veterano*. In Chicano lore the status of *chuco* or *vato loco* was earned and not given, or as Richard would say, "tempered slowly by fire and rain," and the *veterano* is esteemed as a street-smart elder, a storyteller, and of course, a survivor because the rest of his peers are dead.

Like the stories of the past there is a moral infused into each tale with street wisdom, for the age impaired wannabe, newcomer, kiddie, and tourist alike. This written collection of humorous stories will keep the reader just as engaged as the oral story. A word of caution: if you doubt the authenticity of the tale, or don't find it funny, keep it to yourself!

TIO ZUCO

1. Nine Ball Tommy

NINE BALL TOMMY owned a pool hall. Tommy was always sharp, always mirror-shined shoes, razor sharp creased peg pants, maroon shirts, and charcoal gray fedora.

Strange green eyes that never looked at you but missed nothing. He wore short sideburns and a mustache and goatee and had a broken nose from a cue stick fight.

Tommy's place had four pool tables with leather pockets and one table that didn't have pockets but a tray for the heavy money cats.

Once a week I would wash, vacuum, and wax his car. It was a '58 copper/maroon half-top. He would pick me up in front of his place and drive to a liquor store and buy a fifth of Cutty Sark. When we got to his pad he would go inside and I would clean his car for three or four hours. When I was through, he would come out, drop the empty bottle in the trash and drive me back to town. Then he would pay me twenty bucks, which was a lotta bread back then. He would wink and say, "Don't spend it all in my place." I was only one of three people who had credit there. He had a .38 Smith & Wesson in a slide holster by the driver's side and a .25 caliber Berreta under the dashboard—also a 12-gauge sawed-off shotgun in the trunk—I found out later.

When I was 12 or 13, I would play hooky sometimes and threaten to smash his door-length window unless he would let me in. He would laugh and say, "I bet you would, too, you little fucker, just stay out of sight." I would sweep the place out, stoke the potbelly stove with coal, brush all the tables clean, and have them ready for the gamblers and money shooters. Tommy ran a little gambling, two-card monte and shit.

Every once in a while he would have me burglarize his place. He would say, "Pull the score right, hole through the roof, jimmy a window, you know what I mean." Then he would make me work like a slave, breaking into his place, and not pay me until he had called the cops, settled with his insurance, and gotten paid. Some fucking friend.

Once I broke through a skylight and jumped on a pool table and landed on an old couple fucking. They were as scared as I was. While they were trying to put their clothes on, I was trying to jump up to the skylight, just out of reach. There was a room in the back with a cot, but these pukes had to screw on my newly brushed felt. I told Tommy, "I ain't brushing that table no more—cum stains, rug burns, and who knows where those people have been." He thought that was pretty funny, but he put a new felt on it anyways.

That back room was bad news for me anyways. I broke in there once and there was a full-length mirror on the back of the door, and when I opened it there was a guy with a gun pointed at me a few inches away. It was me in the mirror and I almost shit square bricks through a round asshole. I tell you truly, I froze for a second and sweated bullets. I had almost shot myself in the mirror. Have you ever been shot in the mirror? Not even once? And mother-fucking Tommy thought it was hilarious, but he gave me a bonus anyways.

Probably because I had a gun pointed at him from a few inches away.

2. From a Barred Window Revisited

THERE WAS A DOUBLE MURDER trial going on in the courtroom upstairs. A group of vatos were doing time and were bored and didn't even have a drink. Sometimes a friend would bring us a flat of wine or even a couple of quarts of beer through a rear window.

Upstairs in the courtroom the people were quiet and solemn. Suddenly there was a piercing squeal like a pig being grabbed by a big cat. It was my friend Rocky Octavo, who could imitate a pig exactly. It was the middle of July and it was very hot so the courthouse windows were open and the court was directly above the jail. Well, everybody started laughing their ass off and the judge couldn't control them—banging his gavel, yelling "Oder in the court". The jury had tears running down their cheeks; even the murderer was rolling on the floor. So the judge who dressed badly and was an illiterate puke ordered the cops to come down to the jail and kick our ass. But when the cops came down we were all asleep. So after a while when things had settled down Rocky again started squealing like a pig and the shit started all over again.

3. Shooting at and Getting Shot by Friend or Foe

*As told to Tio Zuco By Torito James,
Alias Two Time Jimmy,
Alias Slipper T., Alias Etc., Etc.*

JESSIE T. WAS A SOLID NUMBER I did time with years ago. When we got out, I would visit him down south. We would hang around, have a few drinks, jive around with chicks, and have a few laughs.

He introduced me to some friends and I made a few connections. I started going down there with my investors and my coin and a few guns, and come back with pillow cases full of mota. All the cats down south were cool. But eventually you run into a jive ass who thinks he can burn you. Bad mistake!

My friend and I had just scored a couple of keys and this puke wouldn't deliver. My partner and I easily hunted him down to a motel since he was a 250 lb. pig. While Jessie went up the side stairs, I went around the back, guns ready. Suddenly I saw this giant shadow looming over me and as I looked up he fired. If I hadn't moved, he would have shot me in the head. But he missed and hit my shoulder. Just then my bro shoots him three times and the puke falls over the balcony rail. Now I'm watching this pig's shadow get bigger and bigger coming straight down on me. This giant vomit is trying to kill me even after he's dead.

I barely jump out of the way and he lands right by me

with a splatter and a plop like a watermelon dropped from the third story, which is what he looked like anyways. Now this swine had breath that would knock a buzzard off a shit wagon. He had a tattoo around his neck that had little dashes which said underneath "cut along the dotted line." I never had the chance to slice the bastard but having done our good deed for the day by having rid the community of this garbage pile, it was time to split.

Now I'm shot and the bullet goes in my shoulder and out my armpit. It was just a .25 but at close range it can be a very bad kitty. When the bullet first hits, you just get numb, then cold, then your brain tells your body that you have a red hot slug inside and you scream after you can catch your breath. The shock knocks out your breath and leaves you gasping for air like a fish out of water.

My friends get me the fuck out of there. They take me to a girl's pad out in the desert and some fool pours a generous amount of tequila on my wound and I scream even higher. Then a medic comes and gives me a shot. I get a fever and sleep for three days. I finally make it home a little stunned but with my heavy load intact.

When I was in my fever daze, I dreamed I attended the hog's funeral. His chick was there telling the crowd what a lovely pig he was and said he was probably looking down right now and smiling on them, but having known the puke for what he was he was more likely screaming up from down in hell where even the Devil didn't want to associate with him.

So roast in hell, Piggo, and learn how it feels to be burned like you burned so many righteous people.

4. The Last Run of a Diehard Chuco

MY FRIEND CHICOTE sent his 13 year old daughter Fatima a bag of grass in the mail to her school. Pretty stupid, huh? We warned him. We all told him how stupid and dumbass and illegal it was.

But he said, "she's old enough to smoke shit and I'm starting her off right."

Four of us vatos had just scored some mota from Spañia and we were smoking joints and drinking beer. Chicote suddenly says "I'm sending my daughter a stash of this shit."

We had a good laugh and then realized he was serious.

He had been divorced recently and didn't know his girl's address but he knew the name of the school in her new town.

Nothing we would say could change his mind. We tried humor, sarcasm, and reason.

Nothing worked.

Then a wise ass told him he didn't have the balls to do it. That pissed him off and he splits saying, "you'll see."

Well, a couple of weeks slide by and we had all forgotten this nonsense when some cats drop by my pad and tell me Chicote has been busted. And I say "I'm not surprised. Did he sell tokes to some jive hippie?" Which he was always doing.

And they say "No. the dumb bastard really sent his daughter the mota."

He had sent his girl a baggy of grass in a box of candy care of her school. And the nosy rat bastard principal had checked it out and found the stash. Then he calls the girl into his office and told her "We got a present for you in the mail from your father," and showed her the bag.

And the chick says "Well, that's my Dad." So the piggy principal who had no humor, personality, imagination or soul called the cops. And they in turn called the cops in our town who put the sad-assed fuck in the slam.

The DA, lawyers, judge and cops couldn't believe this guy—and neither could we.

So they finally decided not to jail him. A fucking miracle. Instead they put him in the nuthouse where he got the inmates high with some grass he got during a visit.

Some say his daughter visited him and slipped him some of that bad-assed weed. We'll never know since they're both gone to memory and memories are like dust in a dead man's hand.

P.S. Chicote means *whip* as in *smart as a whip*.

5. Snake Gun Story

THERE WERE ABOUT EIGHT VATOS in this chick's place. Eight guys and about three chicks from different towns but everybody was cool. All the cats had guns but no problem. We're hanging around waiting for the connection, just having drinks and rapping. I was standing at a marble top bar and there was a guy and chick sitting on a couch.

When suddenly from across the room a guy yells "Watch out" and pulls a gun and starts firing. He had seen a fucking snake gliding silently behind the guy on the couch, right behind his neck.

It was a python about three or four feet long. It was a pet belonging to the chick of the house.

All of the guys started firing—me, too. Bullets flying everywhere. Shell casings plinking off the bar marble top and pieces of fucking snake sticking to the wall and the chick runs in from the kitchen crying "My Baby!" The bitch had even named it Smoky or some shit.

The whole fucking living room had been shot up. Mirrors broken, pictures smashed and gun smoke and snake parts everywhere. She hadn't mentioned the snake and now she was really pissed and chased us out and the cops on the way. Everyone running for their car except me. I walked through the back door, across a couple of yards and down a couple of blocks to a grocery store and called a cab to a friend's house.

What would the cops have charged me with? Blasting the scales off a stinking snake? Flinging snake gore on a hideous couch? Violently decorating a garish living room with bullet holes? It would have been an improvement.

I was later shocked and surprised to learn we were not welcome at that house anymore. So we had to find another place to make the connection, preferably some place without a snake or other wild life.

Remember, you can't put a price on peace of mind. And you won't believe this but somebody said that that snake was valuable. Well, so is ammunition.

6. Blues for a Night Screen Dancer

THIS IS A WARM AND FUZZY tale of intrigue, budding romance gone terribly wrong, and even a touch of violence for you bullies out there who like that kind of thing.

New Year's Eve of 30 years ago is one I won't soon forget. I walked into this club and on a small stage is a go-go dancer in a tiny miniskirt with big legs and enormous knockers. She gives me a big wink when I pass by and I thought I detected a 5 o'clock shadow. I ask the bartender who the dancer is and he says, "That's Sin-ah - don't you recognize her?" I say, "Wasn't she a guy?"

He says, "Yeah, but she's a great dancer." And she really was. On a table up front are four guys, one is a soldier in uniform home on furlough with three drinking buddies. The soldier's eyes are popping out of their sockets and his tongue is hanging out of his open mouth. The dancer picks up on the soldier and starts dancing in front of him. Undulating like a cobra. Moving with a smooth rising and falling and side-to-side glide. Then starts to rub her goodies in his face and the guy is going wild. He invites her outside to his car and they hurry out.

When they start to wrestle in the back seat, she tells him she likes it in the rear, but he tells her he's not a back door man and reaches under her skirt and suddenly realizes he has a firm grip and a holy hold on what can only be described as a misguided missile. The soldier boy blows up and starts smacking the chick around—she jumps out of the car yelling and runs into the bar sobbing and says that the lame brute has fondled her in all the wrong places and has made her mascara run.

The next instant the soldier rushes in like a man entering a shop full of clocks ticking, with a hammer in each hand intent on accomplishing complete and everlasting silence. His three buddies are laughing so hard they can't even fight back and the dancer is in the corner dabbing at her eyes and looking like a raccoon. Finally, several guys grab the soldier and throw him out into a snow bank full of slush.

What can we learn from this, boys and girls?

Could it be you should watch out who you kiss under the mistletoe or anywhere else?

Because getting tight with some of these kiddies can make your mustache fall off?

Should the soldier boy have gotten a spankin' and a plankin'?

Should the she-he dancer have gotten a severe tongue-lashing?

(Something that would have made her undoubtedly overjoyed.)

Should the three insensitive buddies receive the sting of the lash across their scrawny shoulders?

Alas, these are questions that have bedeviled man since time began.

So next time you are slipping and a-sliding and peeping and a-hiding, take care what you wish for—you just might get it.

7. Ode to a Hollow Hawk

MY PRIMO CHANO the Lip was a ladies' man. He was tall and thin and had a gold tooth and earring. He was the best liar I ever knew—he could lie his way into heaven. He would enter dance contests and almost always win—then he would share his prize magnum of champagne with his dance partner. He could dance better that anyone even when drunk as a skunk. Chicks would fall in love with him and he would rush right out and buy them a ring. He had been married so many times that he had rice marks all over his face.

The last chick he married was named Marianna. His other wives had always been lovely but this one was a Mamasota Babeona that could raise all your aspirations from 50 yards away.

Chano said after his divorce, "Marianna is so lovely she's close to perfection, but her heart is black with greed and she's selfish to the bone, add that to her envy and jealousy and you are left with a cold stone." He told me "I would curse her, but it would reflect on me. She is a glitter girl who will turn to mold but she will dive into the pit by herself. She would swallow the whole world if she could. She uses her beauty to manipulate and jive every man and boy since she was a young girl. But now she has tried to bullshit a bullshitter who wanted a really good lay so he bought her an expensive bauble and rocked and rolled her all night. And it cuts like a knife but she's out of my life, and I thank God everyday that she's gone."

But since beauty is only skin deep you soon learn that

ugliness goes all the way through.

After the divorce poetic justice begin to set in. She fell in love with the bullshitting handsome gambler who beat her, stole her jewelry and sold her up and down the Sunset Strip. I saw her years later and she looked like a hard-ridden ghost. I asked the bartender who she was and he said "That's Marianna the Famous who can give you a disease from thirty feet away and make your mustache fall off." So I bought her a drink and rapped with her for awhile and wondered how I could have worshipped such a goddess from afar and now saw a sad whipped gray girl with yellow eyes whose once magnificent legs were needle marked and who looked like a setting sun.

8. Dora the Cat's Walloping Wizards Magic Wand Contest

COMING BACK from a run down south my partner Brujo said, "Let's take a short detour to this small town and I'll introduce you to some wild friends that will blow your mind." And I thought why not. This guy always knows interesting people in a lot of towns and I had met several people through him.

We got to a small town located in a beautiful green valley by a river between steep treeless mountains and endless prairie. He immediately drove to this three story whore house where we were welcomed by a huge fat woman with a ton of lipstick, powder and paint and the loveliest face you ever saw.

She looked a lot like Shelly Winters who I had always been in love with. Standing behind her was a very tall dark man dressed all in charcoal grey with a perfectly trimmed beard and an ebony walking stick which I knew was a sword cane. They invited us into a huge parlor with a mahogany carved bar and an ivory stand-up piano. Behind the bar were large mirrors and painted murals of nude women cavorting with satyrs who are part human, part goat, and are noted for riotousness and lasciviousness. They were playing panpipes and flutes and swilling wine and I just knew that I had found my true heaven.

Beautiful young girls were drinking at the bar and reclining on sofas. The lovely Madam was "Dora the Cat." Probably because she sometimes carried a big all white cat with green eyes around. Or maybe because she could kick anybody's ass. I once saw her flatten a large man with one punch.

She was very glad to see my partner and she gave us a drink and introduced us to her girls who were dressed like 1880's dance hall girls. What with the bar and girls I felt like I was in a wild west saloon. I asked my friend "Do you think I could stay here forever?" and he said "calm down or I'll throw a bucket of ice water on you and all the chicks will laugh at you." And I said "Fuck it, I don't care, I want to be somebody's love slave." He started laughing and told Dora what I said. She laughed and told me "I like you, I think I could find a job for you. I told her "anything but a pimp, I know a guy who said he wished that he had an older brother who was a pimp so he could have someone to look up to," which made her crack up again.

She tells us, "you boys are just in time for our annual "Walloping Wizards Magic Wand Contest." I stare at my friend questioningly and he whispers "It's a big dick contest" and I still don't understand so he says, "just watch and let Dora know if you want to enter."

The long mahogany bar was cleared and several girls with tape measures signal they're ready. Then Dora tells the tall dark man to bring the contestants out. In march a weird crew of very different men—they are announced by name and number as they line up at the bar. The first one looks like a tall hillbilly from a coal mine, no name. No. 2 is a black cowboy very famous in those parts with a name like "Blanket Chief" for having balled everyone in sight. No. 3 is a short, fat, scarred, dangerous looking bandit also famous called "Swelled Shoes" but not to his face. No. 4 is a burned out looking wino whose name is Poker. No. 5 is a former sea captain turned preacher named Capt. Seasons. No. 6 is a very well dressed gambler type with a devil-headed ivory cane called Sammy Stones for his guts to gamble and duel with anybody who loses and whines, his weapons being Derringers and Bowie Knives—also a long thin steel band coiled around his hat band which could fly and blind you when he tipped his hat at you. "Stones Indeed." Last but not least is a half-breed Indian who looks like he's asleep whose name I didn't catch.

The Grand Prize is a years supply of free jam and booze. All seven girls are betting on their studs to win. Bets are also going around the crowd, the whole place now packed with politicians, crooks, soldiers from a nearby base and even the local sheriff.

Brujo my friend asks me if I want to place a bet but I decline, never having bet on a winnie before.

The bartender sold everyone a last drink until the contest is over and the test begins. All the contestants pulled out their wongs and the crowd is tense with anticipation. Now all the contestants lay their floppers on the bar and the girls start to measure the throbbing penis of their champion. If one goes flaccid the girl shouts words of encouragement or curses the bastard out with shit like "you couldn't get it up with a backhoe you punk." And the crowd is roaring—everybody trying to get a good look, those in the back looking over their neighbors shoulders.

You never saw so many people trying to get a look at a big dick.

There were some very ugly looking kiddies on display at the bar. I think I even spotted one with a tattoo on it. I'm not sure because I didn't want to stare too long and be struck blind.

Some of those monsters were probably against the law in most states. There were hammer heads, serpents with one eye, a long thin one most likely used for peeking through keyholes and a thick round pole which made you wonder what kind of miracle this magic wand could conjure up. A girl told me there was one with a tattoo which read: "Recuerdos de Constantinopla" which translates: "Memories of Constantinople." Lengthwise of course— what did you think? round and round? But she could be jiving.

The girls were crying out their numbers: "Mine's nine and a half" and another chick would say "that's nothing, mine's ten and a quarter" and another chick would say, "That's nothing mine's eleven and a quarter and the crowd would applaud.

Every class of society was represented. Gentlemen brought their genteel wives who would pretend to be shocked but would take notes on the sly. The well hung were really well represented that day. There were huge pickles from 9 inches to the final winner of eleven and a half by Poker the Wino who won by a head.

9. All The Broken Glass

(Adventures From My Bar and Other Fun Games)

THE FIRST SHOT shattered the bottles on the bar. The second ricocheted off an ashtray and hit the picture of a stripper friend and broke the frame.

The punk who started all this shit now started whining and saying, "Please don't shoot me. I'll do anything."

I said. "Really? Will you polish my knob?"

And he says, "Yes, just please don't shoot me."

I say, "What about my friends? You insulted them, too."

He says, "What ever you say, just please don't shoot."

I told one of my vatos, "Get your chick with the camera in here." We have the punk on his knees pose with a plastic sunflower in one hand and one of the guy's flopper an inch from his open mouth. Then we take his picture and another one with an ugly hammerhead an inch away from his ear, the caption reading, "and I'm going to fuck you in your ear so you can hear me coming."

None of the guys really wanted to check his oil, but we made a lot of copies of the two pictures and handed them around at parties and bars including one I personally delivered to his sister who had once ratted on me. I told her, "See what can happen to you if you drop the dime on me?"

Her brother had come into my bar uninvited and had started breaking glasses and insulting everybody and was just being an obnoxious asshole. But then he started feeling up chicks and laughing at everybody.

I told him to chill out and he turns on me and says, "Fuck

you and your bar, I think I'll just kick your ass."

I just told him, "Hold that thought, Mother Fucker." I dashed into my bedroom and got my gun and when I got back he was standing by the bar full of empty bottles and I fired at the ones closest to him. The bottles exploded and I fired again and more bottles shattered, showering the puke with broken glass and he started pleading, "Don't shoot me!"

After the pictures had made the rounds all around town, the vomit had to get the fuck out of Dodge. He had a brother in another city, but I had a lot of friends there and I sent them some pictures of "Mr. Dick Licker" with his backdoor full of grease and a nickel in his hand. My friends spread the pictures around and the puke had nowhere to go—his brother having seen him performing an unnatural act had disowned him and threw his punk ass out.

The last anyone ever heard of him he was down on Skid Row drunk to the tits on cheap wine and starting to flip, flop & fly because even the winos knew all about him.

10. The Girl Who Climbed Me

(Or the Conquering of Mt. Zuco)

SOME YEARS AGO I was visiting my partner the Alibi Kid who lived in a small town down south. He specialized in being a surprise witness for the defense, hence his name. We were having a barbecue in his back yard with maybe twenty people.

Alibi and I were sitting at a picnic table having a beer when I noticed a small girl staring at me and I asked my friend who she was. Alibi says, "That's my daughter Monica, she's three and a half years old. Ever since you've been here she keeps staring at you. She probably finds you very interesting."

I say, "Well, can you get her to stop staring at me? I'm starting to get a little paranoid. You remember when I had paranoia so stiff you could stand it against the wall?"

He just laughed and then I saw the little girl headed my way. Now children have always scared the hell out of me for some reason and I didn't know what to do. When this scary child got to our table she started to climb laboriously up to the seat at the table and then on to the top and walked on her little legs straight toward me. My heart started pumping faster and I felt paralyzed. I sat there frozen and this frightening kid reaches me and starts to climb me. She starts at my left shoulder and then grabs hold of my pony tail with one hand and my ear in the other and starts heaving and panting up the side of my head until she reaches the pinnacle with one foot on my aching ear and then heaves a sigh of relief, takes a couple of deep breaths and after having taken in the view of the distant horizon—she should have brought a camera, the rotten brat. She starts to descend down my other side and I'm just glad she didn't plant her goddamned flag on my pumpkin head.

By this time everybody has been watching us and trying not to laugh out loud and ruin the show. Fucking Alibi has tears running down his homely, pock marked face and I can see his wife watching through the window about to piss her pants with laughter because she and her bastard husband have seen this sinister monster child pull this shit before.

Anyways, my friend the mountain climber is now using my pony tail to lower herself down, finally reaches the table and steps on my hand and I'm praying my ordeal is finally over and vowing to myself to never again let anyone take advantage of my good nature.

And this child looks me right in the eye for about a full minute as if to say, "Well, don't you want to share your good fortune with your friends?"

And then she just waddles away without looking back, her glad rags askew—never once having said one word—not even a thank you.

And I'm left thinking—Well, just because it never happened doesn't mean it's not true.

11. Of Cops, Corruption and Sweet Revenge

THERE WAS A REAL PIG who thought that he was Wyatt Earp and liked to bully young guys and would steal their beer and harrass them for parking with their girls and making out.

He would break up fights in bars and dance halls and keep their guns and blackjacks, brass knuckles, etc. He would also stop chicks and threaten to ticket them if they didn't put out. Some of the chicks had to give this puke some jam because they had young kids or low-paying jobs they didn't want to lose. He also pushed around helpless winos, whores and even elderly people.

Not all the cops were pigs; of course, some would give an old man who was drunk a ride home or stop a fight and tell you to get off the streets without jailing you.

Getting back to the piggy who thought he was a gun-hawk—he was always practicing a fast draw. One afternoon while walking down a long hall when he thought he was alone he started doing his fast draw bit. I was watching him through a small hole that was drilled in a door that faced down the hall. He would walk a few steps, and then stop and draw his gun. About the third time he drew the gun, he shot himself in the foot. Then he started yelling and screaming and hopping up and down and cursing like, wow.

The shot had made a lotta noise and echoed and re-echoed up and down the hall. Now the sheriff came out of his office, his face red with anger, and gave him such a tongue lashing in two languages and kicked him in his hemorrhoids and then kicked him again from nuts to butt and demoted him to meter maid, took his gun away and made him cry.

I almost felt sorry for the bastard, but remembered what a puke he was. I had been describing everything to the rest of the cats in jail and they were laughing and started a celebration right away.

After the shooting incident, the piggy started sinking lower and lower. One of his last duties was during election time. He was sent out to round up all the winos, take their bottles away and jail them for a few hours, then release them to go vote, telling them to vote for the sheriff. After the poor winos had voted for the sheriff several times, the piggy would jail them again, after giving them a little drink (from their own bottle, of course).

By now everybody had heard the story of the fast draw and the piggy had become a lame joke. But his story was not over. He had become a mean drunk and was hassling the street cats and everyone else even worse.

Then a very hip vato who was always into everything told me about a score and asked if I wanted in. I said, "Fuck yeah, just let me know when."

Now, Mr. Greedy Piggy had accumulated over the years quite a collection of weapons that he had stolen from people he had busted, and had them stashed in an old footlocker under a bed. So we waited until he went to work one night and like true night hawks entered his unhappy home and ripped off his stolen guns, knuckles, knives, blackjacks and a small leather bag of old rare coins. After the great burglary the pitiful piggy went around offering a small reward, but since he had nothing but enemies, nobody knew a thing.

The last time I saw him he was rooting in a dumpster

for day old bread. Perhaps, even though the cold-rayed dawn promises a brand new day he knew his life led down a darkness road, finally having reached the last link of corruption on the long chain that stretches down to a yawning grave.

12. Ronnie the Rat's Innovative Dance Gig

SPEAKING OF BURN ARTISTS who think they can pull jive on you and smile in your face.

I was having a drink when I saw passing by my friend Rose-a-lee and I called her in for a drink and after a couple of beers we went to another bar and the first thing I see is Ronnie the Rat with two chicks. Now Ronnie the Rat was a good looking singer and guitarist who conned everybody including me. I had fronted this vermin $80 bucks of hash and grass and never a payment and here he is buying drinks for 2 broads. They have a couple of drinks and split. The bar is boring so Rosie and I split too.

When we get to another bar here's Ronnie Rat and his chicks. They shoot pool, have a drink, and split. After a half hour Rosie and I do too.

We go into this third bar and there is the Rat and his babes. After a while he passes by to the john and smiles at me. I follow him to the john and he's against the urinal and says, "How do you like my babes?"

I say, "Your babes have calluses on their backs and it's not from starch on their sheets. Where the fuck's my bread, man?"

He says, "Lighten up man, you'll get it."

I say, "When, motherfucker? You can buy two chicks drinks all over town and not even a dime note for me?"

So he laughs and pulls out a $100 bill and waves it in my face and says it's for his ladie's drinks. I pull a .22 automatic and show it to him and he laughs again and says, "Fuck you.

Wait for your bread."

I grab the 100 and say, "You owe me $80. Consider the rest interest," and shoot him in the foot. He starts to hop, skip and jump and yell, scream and holler and is inventing a new dance craze called the shot in the foot boogie, and I'm rolling on the floor laughing my ass off and holding my sides and can't stop. Have you ever fired a gun in a big bathroom? It makes a mighty big noise. I know the cops are coming but I can't stop laughing till Rosie pokes her head in and says, "What the fuck are you doing? Let's go."

When we go out the bartender is gone along with the two chicks and everything is still and quiet except for Ronnie the Fuck's screams. We run in Rosie's car and she says "Where to?" I say "Ruby's", a bar across town where we park in back, have some drinks and ribs with Ron the Man's bread and toast his generosity.

Before we left I told him, "If you ever ask me for anything I'll shoot your other foot and your stinking dingleberries. So if you think you have skid marks on your drawers now, if you push the wrong buttons again, I'll bury you out in the sand."

I heard he moved to Arizona for his health. Being a singer he's probably singing the blues and dancing with a left footed limp.

I leave you with the lyrics from a Bill Haley and the Comets song:

"See you later alligator
After while crocodile
Can't you see you're in my way now
Don't you know you're not my style?"

Merry Christmas and Happy Shooting.

13. Tio Zuco's 24-hr. Barred Window Joint Sales and Emporium

ME AND MY FRIENDS were doing a little time. Some judge, who smelled of deodorant and was a bald-headed chicken fucker with no front teeth, had given us two weeks for some nonsense.

In jail was a trusty—just a kid who was very green and who had a room to himself and was mostly free to come and go. One afternoon, all the cops were gone, and he was searching around and had found an evidence drawer full of marijuana, and he didn't know what it was. He showed me a small amount and I told him to get me more and tell no one. Later, a brother came to the window and I told him to bring me cigarette papers and spread the word that I was holding some bad shit.

There had been a bank heist a month before, and when a posse had been chasing the robbers, they had stumbled on a marijuana plantation. The evidence shelf was just a flimsy affair, easily opened. My friend was back in a flash with another guy with bread. I started selling joints through my newly opened walk-up window. I employed everybody: my two friends, rolling joints; my trusty buddy, bringing me handfuls of grass; and me, dealing with the kitties at the window. I made a killing with my grass and bought friends and fellow inmates groceries and smokes.

And my new friend, the trusty, was my friend for life.

The whole town had been completely dry and now everybody was humming high and my trusty friend and I were rolling in bread. What can I say? I'm here to help.

(My friend, the trusty, went on to own a limousine service and any time I would visit his city, he would drive me around everywhere.)

When I got out of jail, I bought a couple of six-packs, and when I got home my cousin Louie had just arrived from another town. We had a couple of beers and then he had to visit a friend. He had a lovely chick with him—the kind of chick when you say hello is stuck for an answer—but she had the biggest puppies you ever saw. So Louie says, "Here, Tio, have a whore." Now I ask you, how many brothers can give you a beautiful whore when you're fresh out of jail?

But, alas, my friends, your Tio Zuco's tale does not end well.

(I've been waiting my whole life to use the word "alas" even though I don't know what the blue-eyed fuck it means.)

Anyway, after enjoying my friend Louie's gift and doing the diddle bop all night like young doggies, I'm feeling great. A couple of days later I'm walking down he street when suddenly I feel a giant bite on my nuts—the bitch had given me some lousy lice. But I was appreciative because they were imported—having come all the way from Sacramento. My good friend Louie had also mentioned the antidote.

He said if you ever get the crabs, you should get a double shot of whiskey and a handful of sand. First you dump the whiskey on your groin, then wait a little while and pour on the sand, and when the crabs get drunk they stone each other to death. Or another way is to shave half your pubic hair, then pour a little gasoline on the hairy side and set it on fire and when the chatos run from the forest fire you stab the blood-thirsty mother-fuckers with an ice pick.

These things were also special in another way—they were shaped like little Volkswagens and had very hard shells. I would shoot them with a .22 Derringer and the bullets would just ricochet off.

Remember, a vato loco is tempered slowly by fire and rain, even though I once heard a guy boast that when he was born he came out with a joint in one hand and a switchblade in the other, but I find that a little hard to believe.

Lady luck is a fickle bitch, ain't she? Beware of glitter girls who turn to mold.

Please pray for your Tio Zuco and his mission in life.

14. Ballad of the Golden Spike and the Atomic Hurl

MY NEIGHBOR FILAS invited me to go with him to a city as a favor to score some mota for a couple of guys who I'll call YoYo and Bobo. *Filas* is Spanish for *blades* cause my friend could throw a knife across the room and hit you from 30 feet away. A silent art that he taught your Tio Zuco which has saved my life a couple of times. I would practice with him and we would put playing cards on a fence and he could hit the ace of spades in the middle.

Anyways, we went to this town but nobody was holding so on the way back we stopped in this other town and no one had anything either but this cat told us about a guy in this village up in the hills who always had something. We got to this place in the mountains and met this far out cat with long hair which no one had in those days—this vato had tattoos all over, even one which was the letter W tattooed on each butt cheek, and when he bent over it would spell WOW. I didn't have the honor of seeing it but heard about it later.

This vato had an eye patch and wore a wide purple sash with a huge pistol stuck in it. The cat says he doesn't have any grass but can sell us a shot of smack. Filas and I say we don't fuck with needles but we'll ask Frick and Frack if they want some. Now these clowns are rich and arrogant so they want to impress this heavy vato that they're hip. So they roll up their sleeves and the vato introduces the golden spike to the virgin vein and these kiddies get hit like a ball peen hammer behind the ear and sing out like Little Richard's "A

WOP BOP-A-LOO-BOP A WOP BAM BOOM."

Next their eyes roll back and they start to sweat and I know they're going to be sick. The dummies' systems are not used to this garbage and I know they are about to do the Atomic Hurl. I tell Filas, "Let's get the fuck out of here before these punks do the Rainbow Yawn and this badass pirate makes us walk the plank." Thank God there is a liquor store across the street so we buy a case of beer and split, making sure to thank our gracious host for providing us with this wonderful entertainment.

Now we're cruising home and the dumbass twins in the backseat start with the psychedelic gargle—they roll down their windows and stick their heads out and throw up like young doggies and repaint the back part of the car with some very wild colors. They are sweating from their hairline to their toesies and tears are running down their face and one of them is saying, "Take me now, Lord. I've got nothing else to throw up except my underdeveloped testicles." And Filas and I are drinking beer and laughing our ass off.

When we get to the outskirts of our town, there is a bar called Ruby's where we park in back and tell Mutt and Jeff, "You are on your own, boys, and don't think it has been a slice of heaven 'cause it hasn't. Between the stink and the paint job we hope you got everything you got coming to you."

Another time these same beauties went to a city looking to buy a couple of pounds of grass, but were too stupid and too cheap to pay me to score for them since they'd never had a connection. They're rolling down the street and spot a guy standing around that they think is a vato so they call him over and ask him if he can score them a couple of pounds of mota and the cat says, "You're in luck. My brother-in-law just got back from Mexico with a couple of keys." So they go to this house and the guy says, "Give me the bread and wait for me 30 to 45 minutes." They give him almost $400 and the guy goes to the door and knocks. A guy answers. He goes in and these chumps wait an hour and finally one of them goes to the door and asks for the guy. The guy from the house says the guy had been a friend who came to his door and asked for a glass of water and split through the back door.

The dummies start yelling that they gave this guy almost $400 to buy grass and are really pissed. The other guy says he does not know anything about any grass and that they better split before he calls the cops. So Rack and Ruin come home broke but not any wiser.

I partied with some cats from this town later who told me the cat the fools gave the money to was being hunted by some very bad vatos who he had burned and by the cops who had a warrant for his arrest. The hunted guy had hopped a bus to L.A. to visit his brother where he bought new threads and took his brother and his wife night clubbing and was spending coin like WOW.

Don't tell me that God doesn't have a weird sense of humor.

15. The Rocky Roads of General Hogwash

(Lowlifes in my life)

WHEN THE GENERAL Hogwash was discharged from the army for incompetence, he immediately began to order his brothers and friends around. He had only been a private but thought he was pretty heavy. Having served in the military myself I knew the discipline and rules so when he started to give me orders I just told him "Fuck you and your jive orders, Sir."

He tried to manipulate people all the time. Some gullible people would actually believe his dumb shit.

Once at a party he staggered and fell, pretending to be having a heart attack moaning "my heart—my heart." A chick with big titties grabbed him to her chest saying "oh, my poor baby, let me hold you" which is what the punk wanted all of the time. After pulling this shit a couple of times the chicks got hip and said "Fuck you and your punk heart, Mother-fucker."

Once we were riding around when this puke yells "stop the car." The driver slams on the brakes and asks, "What the fuck you doing?" And this jive mother says "that song on the radio, let me out to dance!" The driver yells "you dickhead, I thought it was an emergency" and the fool says "it was!"

A couple nights later we're riding around again and the vomit yells "stop the car-stop the car", just because a great rock song comes on the radio this fart wants to dance, so the driver reaches across and yanks open the door and pushes dancing boy out of the car at 50 m.p.h. into the slush and the snow and we watch him tumble and roll like the true dancer that he is as he disappears into the distance in the rearview mirror. Like a dirty snowball.

One of the chicks starts to cry, "Oh, my poor hunny bunny, go back and pick him up. He might be hurt. Suppose a pack of wild dogs finds him with his skinny ass sticking out of the snow and chew on his hemorrhoids and we'll never be able to do the snuggle bunnies again ever more." The driver laughs, "fuck him in the ass. I hope some bikers take advantage of his good nature and bounce him up and down and turn him inside out and twist him into a nude soprano."

Another time this beauty was hanging with a drinking buddy and had been drinking cheap tokay wine and beer for three days and ended up in a dance hall drunk as a skunk. The cat notes that his friend is at the other side of the bar, so he sneaks out leaving him behind and heads for his buddy's house where he creeps into his friend's home and proceeds to climb into the bed where his friend's wife is snoring away.

Now this kitty has been guzzling garbage wine and beer for days and smells like a sewer and can knock a buzzard off a shit wagon. The chick smells this rotten vermin on top of her, wakes up, starts screaming at the top of her lungs, scared, weirded out and really pissed off. The neighbors wake up, grab shot guns and pitchforks, and wonder who the fuck is being molested in their peaceful neighborhood at this ungodly hour.

This jive mother snaps that the jig is up and starts to dress, leaving most of his rancid wardrobe behind. With luck he makes it to the car with a howling mob carrying torches, hoping to roast his withered testicles on a hot wire. The kitty realizes his number has run out and takes off for a distant village where he is not known.

Now he knows he is being hunted by his friend whose

car he stole, by the cops for being stupid, and several other people hoping for a reward. He finally calls his brother to pick him up and while passing through a small town decides to burglarize a dry cleaners, but they made so much noise they woke up the town's only cop who busted their dumb ass and had his picture taken with these two clowns while also getting praise and honors for having made the town's only ever arrest.

Even the newspaper statewide made fun of these chumps. The headlines screaming in giant print. "Wet Brain Suckers Caught in Cleaners with Pants Down." What were they going to do with other people's clothes?

When they finally got out of the slam, where they had hung around with a bad crowd and been introduced to jailhouse romance and earned the nickname Sugar Drawers.

They go back to drinking garbage wine and start to terrorise holy roller missionaries and get rid of Mormon brothers who go door to door bothering people. So a grateful community at last forgave them.

This saga will continue at a later date because I'm so tired of laughing at the memories of this asswipe General Hogwash, and that is more than a person of my tender years can bear.

P.S. now that he has hung up his Rock & Roll shoes, some dark and stormy night he might be back when you're asleep and squeeze your peaches.

16. A Prayer for Harmony Raine

(Santa on the Rocks)

A COUPLE OF DAYS after Christmas I was having a drink at my favorite bar. I asked my friend Harmony, the bartender, if she had gotten any nice holiday gifts.

She exploded all of a sudden and started screaming and cursing me out, scaring the shit out of me and pissing me off.

I yelled, "Whoa, you cretin bitch, what's with this malediction shit?"

She cools down and says, "I'm sorry, I just hate Christmas and you hit a sour note."

I say, "I was just trying to make conversation, I didn't mean anything."

She says, "Let me explain. When I was a little girl my mother took me to a department store Santa in my hometown, Chicago. I begged her not to take me because my dad had taken me to a circus when I was five years old and the clowns had scared the hell out of me. I was frightened of people in weird costumes, but mothers being the assholes that they are, she forced me to go and sit on this rat bastard's lap. I could see through his fake beard and he started to breathe his halitosis and whiskey sour vomit gas in my face and I started to cry and pissed on his lap.

The red-nosed bum lets out a roar and knocks me on my ass to the floor. The women in line with kids are watching this violence and begin to swing their purses at fucking Santa and children are crying and the manager calls on another Santa to control the first Santa who gets punched in the nose for his trouble and gets up and proceeds to kick the first Santa in the nuts.

Santa number 1 pulls a gun and fires a warning shot, shorting out the lights on a giant Christmas tree, starting a fire and the ricochet shatters a plate glass window causing panic but also opportunity for thieves to grab anything in sight.

Customers are stealing and fighting with security guards and cops are pulling up in squad cars pouring into the store trying to stop the riot. Paddy wagons drive up and cops are arresting Santas with black eyes, women swinging purses, and thieves running away with gift-wrapped goodies.

People are beating the shit out of cops and each other in front of TV cameras and having a holiday to remember. My mom by now is hauling me home and yelling at me for having caused a wrecked store and fucked up everybody's holidays and I'm saying, "Fuck you, I told you I didn't want to go."

Well, this war was televised across the country—then across the world, with people in Islamic countries saying to each other, "See, I told you these Christian fuckers really know how to celebrate the birth of their god."

Harmony the bartender says, "Now do you understand why I hate Christmas?"

And I say, "Yeah, I can dig it, thanks for making me see it your way."

Note: The first Santa didn't really pull a gun. I just threw that in for flavor. But if you can dig it, its yours for New Year's.

So jingle bells to you and your shiny hiney.

17. Humito's Strange Revenge

(Feathered Friend Blues No. 3)

HUMITO WAS AN OLD MAN I met in jail many years ago. We were friends for a long time and I was saddened to learn he had died recently.

First of all, his name means "Little Smokes" in Spanish. I never knew his real name. He always rolled tobacco cigarettes and joints perfectly. The two of us were in the Calendar Hole alone and my friends brought me flats of wine and quarts of beer through a rear window. We made a funnel out of a magazine cover and my cats would pour the wine into one jar and the beer into another jar, the beer turning into foam for awhile. I got my new friend drunk as a pig and we sang dirty songs and told stories and he told me this far-out tale:

"I've been a mechanic and inventor for years. I went to a dance and picked up a whore and fell in love. Pretty stupid, huh? Happens to all of us. Well, I treated the bitch right but she left me for a pretty boy punk. I was pissed off but what could I do? Fight a guy twenty years younger and thirty pounds heavier for a slut?

"But, one day, while walking to the park, I passed by this guy's house which was right by the street. Looking into his window, I saw my whore sitting by this guy on a couch while his mother and father and two other men were playing cards on the kitchen table. That summer was very hot and these people left the window open for fresh air.

"In my backyard I had a bunch of bird feeders and I invented a trap to catch birds. Soon I had a wire cage full of all kinds of birds. There were robins, crows, hawks, chickadees, and so on. One beautiful moonlit night I stalked like a true nighthawk up to this puke's open living room window and opened my cage full of very angry birds into that tranquil, peaceful setting and kicked back to watch the fun. I slammed the window shut and giggled at my Chicano ingenuity.

"The pissed-off birds were disoriented and attacked everything in sight—flying into the lovers on the sofa, onto the card players, knocking over some lit candles on the fireplace mantle, setting the curtains on fire, and breaking every fucking dish in the cupboard.

"Smoke is now fucking with the birds and people are in panic, with me looking in approval at the mayhem that can only come from a job well done. I'm rolling in the dirt with laughter at the bitch beating up pretty boy, card players being pecked by angry hawks and bluebirds, and dogs and cats trying to get the fuck out. With rat-bastards coughing their lungs out, birds shitting all over, I stagger home satisfied and my anger gone.

"The next day I'm sitting on my porch drinking coffee after having filled my bird feeders in appreciation. Some cops show up and say that pretty boy's mother told them 'It has to be that jealous Humito. He's the only one that could think this shit up.'

"When the cops tell me this story I start to laugh in disbelief and soon the cops are cracking up, too. So I invite the cops in for a drink and give them a tour of my garden full of bird feeders and remind them to always remember that our feathered friends are here to help."

So the next time someone says to you "Who?" you tell them "Who, hell. You ain't no owl. You don't shit through no feathers."

18. The Gateways of Oblivion

(It has been a good run!)

SOMETIMES we think we deserve another season to slide—who do you think you are? Special—your shit don't stink?

So check out your past numbers. Mind the Truth—don't put flowers on your memories.

A jive mother jumper who tries to pull a gypsy switch does not have a reflection in the mirror.

When you're down to the seeds and stems and the wick on your glower is shaking low maybe your last link has been reached and your free flower balloons are floating away into that vast vermilion sky.

Just when you're pouting about your Righteous pain and you are certain someone is punking out on your score, the light of time floats in and makes you pick up that you have no kick coming and that dues are not for sale to a hustler.

Tell me truly—do you really know every bartender and street chicken on the flying floor? Or perhaps there are tickets to run in the burning evening light—I'd go for the old time juke box stroll because it's everlasting.

To some there is a very narrow line between humor and ignorance. Neither do they know the difference between a sucker and a friend—weird, huh? Perhaps in anger I am spilling about myself but I am a vato and have no reason to lie.

We all pay dues eventually. But mine are superior to yours in the rain. Or?

I once wrote:

The Destiny that guides you is a long and piercing lance that's shining like the good luck charm that's dangling from the mirror in a Trance.

19. PARABLE
God and the Devil Fighting over Me

(Quarrel)

God: I ain't taking this motherfucker, give my place a bad name.

Devil: Bad name? You voted for Hitler and now voted for The Donald and have been known to enjoy Michael Jackson's music—a flaming faggot child molester fairy playing in your heavenly room.

Remember the jive number we had when you said Heaven was full and you didn't know what he was—White-Black-Man-Woman and you wanted to slide this puke on me. I didn't know either—My Hell was clean, this vomit would darken my place.

What would my clients think?

Atilla, Nappy, Genghis, Hitler and other vomits–they might fucking go the wrong way.

Cats and chicks were getting fierce on my case.

Judas was beside himself—Catherine of Rainford-by-the-Sea threw a silver stiletto at my head right between my horns—you Bastard.

God: So am I a bastard—with me an accident of birth. But you Sir, are a self-made man.

Thank u

Thank u
for the gift that lasts a lifetime
Thank u
for the years of growth and realization
for the path of light that leads
down darkened
stairways
In the hall of age and the door of
time stands still
Is eternity forbidden behind the door
Does the feel of creation
steal away
To a cellar of ignorance and scorn
There is love—there are friends
in imagination.

There's the tightening
Of the bracelets
And the pictures
And the prints
Then abuse, humiliation and
Intimidating hints
And if you talk back
To the bully
He'll billy club you to
Your knees
All of this and more
Awaits you
When the Captain gets the keys

In the Kangaroo courtroom
The judges and the lawyers
Go through motions of deceit
Now the assassin in you awakens
As you flare at their conceit
Well, they grin as their
Gloved hands
Reach for their tainted fees
And the Captain in his coffin
Keeps hanging to his memories
An' me, I still got the Monkey Bite Blues
Since the Captain stole my keys.

The Monkey Bite Blues

(Or the Captain Kept the Keys)

Trying to con a con
On the High C's
Jiving with the Man
That the Captain has the keys
Stealing from the stranded
Hiding behind the badge
My watch—my knife
My money and My peace
I've got the Monkey Bite Blues
Since the captain got the keys.

Your belongings disappear like smoke
An' to them it's just a joke
Around the campfires they
Still tell the stories
About how they keep
From going broke
From the time that they
Yell "Freeze"
To when the Captain gets the keys

The Merchant of Dreams

You the fool that gathered the snow
It was laid there for many a reason

But that's something you never shall know
You can fly for only a season

Virgin veins that velvety flow
They're cleaning the stables this season

So your mind they surely will know
Now the candles that witnessed your treason

Heathen horn lamps that flicker and glow
Humanity's snares that brainwashed your vision

False friends sleep while whistling winds blow
Stormy birds of time sit mocking your mission

Echoes asking formula for friend or foe
From you the empty fool that gathered the snow.

Ode to the Cat

(Oda al Gato)

Hidden knives switchblade fast—Night Eyes
Beauty cloak—stealth and stalk—Night Eyes
To blink at fire—to sleep and stretch—velvet lies
A lion's walk—a leopard's breath—Night Eyes
African veldt Eden sunrise

There was a god who dreamed a leopard made of snow
Kilimanjaro
A hunter since birth through mouse hole carpet
Or where Jaguar jungles grow

The golden eyes—the patient purr
The savage fight—the blinded cur
An' through all this he'll let you know
You were the master—you were the slave
And you who took—
Well, who now gave?—Night Eyes.

A Dreamer's Question

I can't seem to find no doctor
That I can tell my troubles to
No, I can't seem to find a doctor
That I can tell my trouble to
An' every time I think about you
I get so blue through and through

There's a time when you're above me
An' there's a time when you're not there
Say, there's a time when you're above me
An' there's a time when you're not there
There are times I think you love me
An' there are times when you don't care

An' I just wish that you were standing
Where you think a prisoner mourns
Said, I just wish that you were standing
Where you think a prisoner mourns
Now there's no love that's more demanding
Than to reach for flowers through the thorns.

Parables and Mirrors

Drinking up a lifestyle—looking for the key
Bite out of the apple—serpent on a tree
Wind up in a cell block staring at the walls
Bars on the windows—scrawled message on the halls
Rules and regulations—dusty carpet of olive pits
and blue
Meals of strangulations—medicines that think for you

Put a coin in the juke box
background music that's ignored
Conversation dullness—bourbon on the rocks
Bar stools and ashtrays—hollow eyes so bored
Won't you have a drink on me—a splash of that or this
The hell with your liver—it'll come out in the piss

Then the tune of blinding headaches
And the lurching through the fog
Wake up falling in the abyss
And then the final sleeping like a log.

Visions of Michael Blind

Michael Blind lived alone
in a cave in a canyon
An' dreamed that he rode through the
clouds on a fire-breathing stallion
He looked down on grey gloomy cities with
their cloud crowns of fume poisoned smoke
To him they resembled square prisons where
life is just a plastic card numbered joke

He flew over rivers and streams once life
giving, sparkling and slime free
He felt shivers and heard screams smothered
in soap suds, grime and ashen algae
The tarnished beauty of nature—what a price
one must pay for what he cannot see

He cruised above mountains, valleys and hills
where erosion carries away what it kills

Said Michael Blind to his fiery steed:
"See what Man does with a heart full of greed
He poisons the air that he breathes, pours
death on the waters and dissolves his own land
It's my world he's destroying—how much
more before we take a stand?"

Fortune Teller Baby

(Sheila's Blues)

She keeps sticking to her lies
She's just a surface rider in
a stone disguise
Well, that Fortune Teller Baby, you're
so blind, but she's so wise

With legs that reach way up to Heaven
An' deep peach kisses down, down to Hell
Yes and Well, that Fortune Teller Baby
Just keeps smoking in your shell

There's that Fortune Teller Baby
on a street corner lookin' nice
Well, she's selling those vice legs
and lips of ice
With your money in her pocket
and her sickness in your eyes
Cause there's always one who sells
and one who buys.

Gallery Town

(Tano's Bar)

That moneyed gringo greed keeps eating
Away at my once lovely Gallery Town
This plague of strangers seems to swallow
up everything even if nailed down
Bells that once rang out with laughter
toll with sadness at sundown
And the Indian—and the Spanish
and the Artist of Renown
They all seem to feel the stillness
As their beauty slowly drowns
In this gamble of a tombstone
That they call Gallery Town

So every time a passing stranger
Returns your smile with a frown
Just remember that there's a difference
Between being white and being brown
And that their justice just keeps melting
In favor of Gallery Town
But now there's a sinister aroma
The stern features of a clown
That's sneering at the foolishness
of an unhealthy joke called
Gallery Town.

To Gods—Tin and Otherwise

Neanderthal thoughts—so far away
now gone
From silent skyships
The twilight ends
The giant yawns
And fur thieves follow suit
Through a green glass glow
The tremble breeze
Casts evening shades

But through all our days
What did we learn?
But to leave
For one night's pleasure
And then once again
Return.

Epitaph

At the end of a scream the child of the
dawn is now born
And throughout all his days among flowers
he remains only a thorn
He escapes in a dream from a world that
is shattered and torn
Ignores the abuse of the fool and the
ignorant faces of scorn
Now at dusk he lies dead with one liar
pretending to mourn.

Crosses: Alone

Crime crosses standing on horizons
of blood skies ... alone
empty now of hatred laughter and
pain filled cries ... alone
clean conscience bystander uninvolved
in accusation lies ... alone
And you my master—you my slave—who now
lives and who now dies? ... alone

To Marie in Motion

But you baby, are but a blanket that can be
Spread out under any shady tree
In the back seat of a limousine
Or in a flop house for a fee
There is circumstantial evidence that
All the members are full of glee
And that the time eroded memories can bring
Their stage fright to your knees

Well, you're a skylight to the heavens
And a mine shaft to your cell
If there is satisfaction to a customer
Can he steer clear of your hell?
You're callous—you're an exit
You are mileage of despair
You're a gallows—an exhibit
You're hard road in disrepair
You are nothing sold for something
You're a consolation prize
You're a wine glass full of vinegar
You're a curse in euphorian disguise.

Of Coins

I like to play with coins
They are usually well rounded
With a head and a tail
Unfortunately they are two sided
Sometimes I wonder if they are earned
Or well spent
The honest labor of love or leaves
Blown by the wind
But the other side of love is pain
And where there was laughter are now
Tears—And until out of the two sided
Coin there is one made whole—
Until then can love and sadness build life.

The Darkness Road

Hooded riders slithering through the
gloomy frightened night
Carrying terror torches held in hate-
filled hands of flight
Fang and claw crusaders of the fiery cross
and quicksand grave
Hoof beats thunder down the darkness
road to brand a man a slave

Behind the symbol of the circle
a band of torture tyrants ride
Fear carried by the wind seems to
make the moon behind a cloud to hide
The savage storm approaches—the winds
of evil howl through your door
In the noose-neck of their victim
the pounding blood is now a roar.

Love Song to a Geritol General

(or Prince Valiant Rides Again)

A country ruled by a senile relic
strutting in vulgar uniforms
Parading medals won in armchair
battles in imaginary warfields
In old age armed with yes men hunting
big game in paper jungles
Still striving to keep memories of
yesteryear warriors' praises
Demonstrating classic examples of
lameness and feeble brains
Wave your banner high
Mr. Wheelchair General.

The Flower Cathedral

On the altar of behavior
There now stands your only son
Just a miniature of blasphemy
And some trophies he has won
They will grow to be comedians
And to serve the swine in bars
Wit and glamour undertakers
Glamorizing fallen stars
But you will always recognize them
Having been one recently
Just time's shadow shifting
Mirrors decently
There will be no answers captured
For they who now serve in turn
They're now chapters—pages numbered
With their zealot booklets burned
Glittering ruins of stale tomorrows
They'll forever shine in shame
Numb the mind with tales of sorrow
That bring hatred to your name.

Blues for Moira

There are mountains of money
And fountains of honey
And you shiver alone in the dark
Oh, where have your friends gone?
All of a sudden there are none
And you freeze to the bone in the park
But there was a time when
The sun rose and fell then
And life was to you but a lark
So will you tell me tomorrow?
There will be no more sorrow
And that their bite will have left
Their death mark.

Orphan Skyways

An' at night you'll wake up screaming
and you'll ask the reason why
In blood puddles your feet struggle
when your highways are the sky

Vanish citizens of fortune—vanish
with your wealth and fame
All your children are now scattered—but
who will they ever blame

Clouds of mushroom monsters building—clouds
that slaughter with no pain
An' the dust of death keeps falling—like
a blind angry god's heat rain

Martyrs cry to you for mercy—mercy not for
just a few
But for freedom from destruction that will
claim your children too

Take your business elsewhere—stranger, do
not bother me by day
An' at night I'll be off wanderin' where no
business can ever pay

In a diary of doomsday no escape is
written first
Why do your children die of drowning while
my children of thirst?

Scenario for Trumpets in June

The fury and lash of the singing winds
Are closing in on a black edged door
Two windows of bright lights
For one old man with his treasures gone
Hanging blue accolades
Temerity trembles because she's been left behind
They will always try to separate them
With time's curtain call
But one cannot forget
And must surely remember
They only call your name who listened
And spoke with other voices
The roar of silence remains your friend
When you have lost the innocence of enemies
But shaking hands and bowing heads
Regard the guardian gate
As sparks of summer thunder
An envoy of disease boxes—bands and wonders
Your call this song remembers
As times own meridian tender
An owl awakes from your cruel works
And shuts her wisdom eyes to your
Fine and glistening splendor.

Kid Fang

(Fourteen Measure of Time)

The condemned man still is waiting
For the coming of the dawn
And the sun that never rises
Cheats the gallows and the gun

The boy that stalks the cellblock
Thinks of bells that never rang
In the crime kingdom of the gang leader
Of the cat they call Kid Fang

In the alleys and the rooftops
Where the hunters stalk their prey
Are the forgotten unbelievers
That choose the games that you will play
Will the steel bars break the dreamer?
Will the law have won the hand?
Will the judges with blind justice
Undertake the leading of the band?

He paces by barred windows and remembers
Songs his dead wife sang
And the guards do time as lonely
As the cold and fast Kid Fang

Now the everlasting sorrow
That just will not go away
Because now there's no tomorrow
Just a wish for yesterday

And the condemned man still is waiting
For the coming of the dawn
And the sun that never rises
Cheats the gallows and the gun.

Sorcerer's Moon

An' now they're looking for you
With a gun
A hunting game to see how fast and
Far you run
And it makes no difference now
What you have done
To them you're just some money
And some fun
Yes, and now they're looking for you
With a gun

There's a die-hard undertaker
And he hums a mournful tune
And he prays they'll bring you back
In time for Sorcerer's Moon

An' now they're looking for you
With a gun
Blood behind a badge now hunts
The father and the son
And vow they'll neither eat nor sleep
Till they have won
And persecute your kind till
There are none
Yes, and now they're looking for you
With a gun.

From the tower to the dungeon—all was laughter
all was style

Now the power of the death knell leaves a mocking
crimson smile

From the parapets to the ice pits you can hear
the ghostly sigh

And the hearse keeps rolling numbly from
the Castles in the Sky

In the mirror dim reflections swiftly still the
eternal cry

Feel the terror of an old age while you watch the
shadows die

Just remember where your past lies
—with the Castles in the Sky.

Castles in the Sky

Children catching phrases—phrases lying idle
in the sand

All the pain that love erases—whip and glove and bridle
trembling in your hand

Children building castles—bastions crumbling with the tide

Waves that sweep with foam and rumble
all of those who try to hide

A time to build—a time to die

But there still floats a light reflection
of those Castles in the Sky

The parade is nearly over—the hooded figure shifts his
dagger on the sly

He's just a death dealer you can buy

He looks like a silent sentry watching the death cart go by

His hooks will deny you entry to the Castles in the Sky

When the Legends Die

From a man into a mannequin
Kill the customs old and strange
Bring the fire flower from the forest
To raise in a golden cage
Still the song of sunlit mornings
Mind their manners—learn the lie
All of this and more awaits you
When the Legends Die

From the old will come forth
A brand new way
And the death of any season brings
The birth of a new day
So will the laughter end the mourning?
And the new born baby cry
Time will test the everlasting
When the Legends Die

Sing sad songs for new beginnings
Learn of pencils and of rules
Heritage of ancient teachers
Change brought on by different schools
Waterfalls of color splashing
On rock hills where eagles fly
Now they're just another sunset
In all this the Legends Die

To Maria

With a necklace of smoke rings
And a key of bright answers
I would search for your doorway
Through this screen of night dancers
Across forbidden bridges of laughter
And down welcome alleys of pain
Still this road runs before me
Through the flames and the rain
Though I stumble through darkness
Lean against walls of despair
I will rise up and follow
Climbing pathway and stair
Until at last I shall sight you
On that ebony chair
And you'll know that I held you
In my soul and the air.

There are numbers with faces
In corner dark places
That are forgotten by all but a few
An' though they separate brothers
From all of the others
Your vanity still will show through
And then at long last
They will bring up the past
And remember just who was the fool—Mr. Cool

Though your future seemed bright
They will put out the light
An' they'll sigh with relief when you're gone
An' though they will bring flowers
And shed tearful showers
You always knew just what made them run
And so was the gem polished?
Or have they demolished?
A jewel—Mr. Cool.

Mr. Cool

With your sentence all served
They got all they deserved
Though the carpet's still stained
By the flood
But they see it all now
They'd forgotten somehow
A reminder that water never weighs
More than blood
But the seeds of the clan
Expose the deeds of the man
Not the tool—Mr. Cool

In the reflection the ghoul
That stares up from the pool
Blows your mind—when you find
That it's you—Mr. Cool

Talons of Fate

Through the night a ghost is riding
seeking out where you are hiding
on the night winds swiftly sliding
coming through the darkness for your throne

You who laughed at people crying
turned your back when they were dying
is it you now who are sighing
wondering why you lie alone?

Now your empire is slowly crumbling
through the fog your mind comes stumbling
and your dream's voice lowly mumbling
that all you now have is your name upon a stone

You who thought could never blunder
has the truth stolen your thunder
is there just a light explosion where your
star once brightly shone?

Where columned temples once stood gleaming
statues proudly towering beaming
is there now a swampy jungle steaming
or in a desert is your muscle now a dusty bone?

Images In The Morning Mist

The Zero cold
Disguised in beauty and splendor
The sorrow ballads mourn
Erasing battlefields
Tinsel triumphs—a foreign hook
The Grand Madame of flame and wonder
Desire and Prayer walk hand in hand
Pages of grass in waves of air
A hollow tomb curls in smoke
Cruelty remains pinned to an iron wall

A cliff of sand can threaten time
Snowflakes in silence descend in rhyme
Stale Scriptures posing with halos
Wires of wood combine the liquid stations
Of evil and of good
The strength of boulders—a mystery force
A path of mud—a gravestone curving
In outer passageways of a cavern's holy song
A timeless soldier sings
Winding bells ring sadness
And then move on
And binding cells create madness
And then move on
And then move on.

Do the swollen streams swim and swirl
And ever higher flow?

Do the peaks release their numbers?
Do the aged infants mourn?

Are these trials and tribulations
A new way of being born?

Will the calm come with the dawning?
Will the raven return home?

Does the storm have new horizons?
Is there crimson on the foam?

Will this be a test of justice?
Or can this be called an act of love?

Is an olive branch still waiting
For the now departing dove?

Tempest Lament In Blue

Did the prophets foretell warnings?
With a staff of wisdom smite the rock

Can you hear the jeer of screaming millions?
Can your ears still hear them mock?

Pride and passion replace mercy
Brains are useless as a tool

Drums and pipes and banners waving
The incredibility of a fool

Now you see the distant flashes
Now the sprinkling of the rain

Soon the darkness will glide over
The ever increasing pain

Does the laughter change to wailing?
Does the understanding dimly glow?

Requiem for a Vato Loco

(Death Watch: Part Three)

The single knight messiah
Who chilled the numbers of the night
With tales of screaming jive maids
That made you want to die of fright
Like strands of sparkling diamonds
That live in contrast to your throat
And your friends who stared in wonder
Now desert the sinking boat

But your enemies tried to tell you
That dreaming was a drag
So now you're listening without humor
soak your feet in a soiled flag
So step aside for stoned stepped warriors
with helmets of bright lights
And their victories crowned in sorrows
in all their battle might

Just the castle walls keep standing
in mockery of your grave
And the silent sermons echo chantings
with smiles of defiance against the lonesome brave

The eulogy is now delivered
By neighbors with trembling hands
So rest in peace my Brother
For I'll join your tomorrows
In the breaking of the bands.

III

A sanguine gallows at sunset
Claims the blind of the temple
Conquerors breed temptations
In the mind of a fool
From the door of a dungeon
Come the rumblings of Hate
Sacrifices of laughter raise
The lanterns of flight
And the last free horizons
Sought by pleas of the Vain
Will now echo through canyons
Of eternity's reign.

Fragments From a Siege

Through a window of noise
Flies the past ever faster
Through a blizzard of ruins
Glide the chariots of Rage
Casting silver and paper
To the priest of Despair
And at last the bells toll
Of a war everlasting
To the tragic magician
Who still prays on the hill

II

There are windmills of Fate
Defiantly standing
A curse and a prayer cry out
Their chain law
Smoldering perfumes drift
Through whispering stones
Carrion sentinels gather
Mist and cloak ashes
And memory prophets
Stifle street screams
Simple warriors and maidens
Dance through passions of time
Parading physicians of sorrow
Wear bracelets of pain

He's been from rags to riches
Loudly stumbles and falls
But he answers quite swiftly
When he answers your calls
Now all the hatred that festers
That you thought would be love
Has become this insanity in a
Wine colored glove

He's the novelty dwarf in
The copper maroon velvet glove
A deformed monster masquerades
As your friend from above
Behind the copper maroon velvet glove
Yes, and now your nightmare grows near
In the shimmering mask and the fire laden glove
The silent killer is all yours as he smothers
Your scream with his
Copper Maroon Velvet Glove.

A Page of Hate

(Theme in Venom)

At the door is a dwarf with a
Copper maroon velvet glove
He checks out your lady
And sneers at your face
His hair is full of grease
And his push comes to shove
He's the poisoned dwarf with the
Copper maroon velvet glove

He's grotesque and obscene as he
Dangles his chain
An' he jumps up and down
While he mangles a dove
The wild drunk in a suit
Wears a maroon velvet glove

You gave good food
And the warm comfort of home
To this blood-eyed
Swamp-dwelling gnome
Now he drools and he shrieks
As he tugs and pulls at the sleeves
Of his masters above
This deceased little man with the
Copper maroon velvet glove

III

A chant of the chain and the lash
A mute witness to the bondage of heathens
Twin downward spirals of heel and brow
Join images of the fountain dead garden
An entrance to the kingdom of thorns
The weight of dire isolation
One last nightmare of the abyss of silence
The descent to the cellars of madness
And in the dungeons of darkness
Find at last the release of Despair.

The Plague of Strangers

Denial of safe passage
Through the curtains of the night
A desolation desert of
Dust and bones and skulls
Where the ghosts of wizards
Stalk through the corridors
Of time eroded temples
Sentinels of wood and feathers mirror
A guardian with claws
Silent altars—idols with halos
Of steel spokes

II

Swarms of agony beasts fly against
Storms of thundering wings
Vast spaces of the hoof and torch
The slashing howl of abysmal terror
A scourge of lamps extinguished by
The horn and the claw
A deluge of dust forms and pillage
The forerunner of the silent shroud
And the unborn wail
A vision's dark portrait from
The disease scorched eyes of a
Prophet and an angel of famine and war

But with you my benefactor
How can there be pain or misery?
Just the passing of the seasons
Winds of Change bring Clarity
Wear a glove when dealing Sorrow
Change False Dreams for Reality
Cash in on the gold rush
Don't let the sand choke your decay
And with Society's Pet Drama
You can garnish all their pay
And then the Mist of Dawn lifts slowly
And reveals that neither you nor I can stay

Still that good luck charm keeps dangling
From the mirror in a trance
And the hum that train was building
Shares the rumors of Romance
But with friends like you—not you—not I
Have got a chance
And the Destiny that guides you is a long and piercing lance
That's shining like the good luck charm
That's dangling from the mirror
              as in a trance.

You would seem a disbeliever
Of the gifts we offer free
Have you ever known the treasure
Of tried and true fidelity?
I can sense that you are bitter
There's a tension in the air
And the cracked mirror on the stairway
Reflects an empty chair
So learn to show appreciation
Violence can't work they say
Just remember what their Trust brings
It can change night into day
And the ache of Love just smolders
For it means well as they say
Then there's the ashes of a friendship
Just a memory that fails
From the harbor or your caring
To the magic screaming nails

And the good luck charm is dangling
From the mirror in a trance
And I wish my enemies could see you
If only a swift and passing glance

In the sermon of the night shade
Truth and lies change quality

Through These Halls of Anger

A good luck charm is dangling
From the mirror in a trance
With friends like you, baby
From a gallows my dreams would dance

The future is paved with good intentions
And your kiss is emptiness
All the strangers who were welcomed
Have proved their worthiness
This is for your own good
I still hear the angels say
Would we lie about directions?
Or would we show you the way?
There's a price for every moment
Of the sunshine of your smile
There's a tax on every dollar
Of your warm and strong hand dial

And the good luck charm is dangling
From the mirror in a trance
And with friends like you, baby
My enemies just wouldn't stand a chance

The humble servant glows with comfort
in a cave of hollow mirth
Saved from true wonderings—too lazy
to wind the hands of eternity's clock
His wife drones on—Madame Monotone
She's colored glass whimpering against
a beauty stone
In the distance new creations even now
are being reborn
And the riders sweep clean the evening sky
New wind carved forms change
ghost like—lightning quick
All trees and willows bend their
heads and nod as unseen shadows pass
Whispers and coins fly—singing thru the sky
A season's fingers tipped with frost
A paintbrush of the cold
But all the things you'll remember stay
Only until their appointed day
And the season of the horsemen shall sweep
the evening sky clean.

Reflections in a Dark Hour

(The Horseman)

Three horsemen sweep the evening clean
Three doorways lead outward to oblivion
An archer stands poised and fires
angry laughter at the question
marks of time
Silence swiftly running—as a hunter
charged with skill and deathly fate
No stumbling stones to hurl narrow
challenges
No loud voices to brag of an ancestor's
plight
Three horsemen sweep the evening sky clean

Silver Strings

(Epistle to an Enemy of Honor)

The hollow hawk is perched on a vinyl barstool
With lines smoother than quicksilver and he
        ain't nobody's fool
Egyptian cigarettes lit with a golden lighter
        he's the ultimate in cool
With one eye on the doorway and one eye on
        your purse
He's the blessing of the ladies—those that
        care to reimburse
With a gold tooth and a rolled wink you would
        never think he'd be a curse

But you're the Prince of Paupers
        You're the whisper of the crowd
You're the question and the answer
        You're the lining on the cloud

He's a butterfly in full bloom—an' he's a
        worm with wings
He's a hunter of the lonely and of happiness
        he sings
Until the elegant parasite is tied to your
        purse strings
Much younger than the woman who was lonely
        in the dark
She makes sure his hand is held while
        strolling in the park
It's a friendship of convenience—bought
        and paid for by the mark

But you're the Prince of Paupers
        You're the whisper of the crowd
You're the question and the answer
        You're the lining on the cloud

Baby Load

What happened to your humor, Baby Load?
I've heard it said your mask's been
Slipping day by day
That your good looks and your future
Seemed to quickly fade away
Is this snake nest just a tumor?
Has the slipshod hit the road?
Or did the makeshift and the bandit
Burn your humor, Baby Load?

Did the circus cancel early?
Did your figure float away?
Are the castaways abandoned
In a casket in the bay?
There's the gas cap—there's the car hop
There's the door to a brighter day
It's a fading dream to weave a winding road
An' did the jester dance with humor, Baby Load?

Your soft smiles that ran with laughter
Memories of yesterday
But there's always love that's blinding
'Till the hills erode away
And the snake pit is now a garden
And the rumors have run the road
They're all patterns of your humor, Baby Load
Just abstract images of humor, Baby Load.

The Night of Two Assassins

From a horde to a handful—a vanishing wave
to a locust alone

Something valued now not spared
in a bare room of a memory snared

Between the bark of a fool
and the gleaming white lie of a jester

From the drumroll of clocks farther grinding
until the collapse of the fear of the snail

From the depths of a fanatic's unholy murmur
to the towering heights of the princes of sleep

Where the lance of the night slashes
through a desert of abysmal terror

Sheltering shields cross the plains of the pen
and only in a shaft can the distance of the echoes
be measured.

Mind Games No. Seven

They come at you out of oceans and beaches
They come at you out of ocean and wave
An' they are the scarlet and the red runner leeches
They smile like a scoundrel and sneer at the brave

And oh, how I'd love to bow down to your graces
Admonish the scruple—and vanish in time
But they who would hold me—now hold all the aces
And would dare decapitate me in my prime

There once was a law that said
you shall burn all the bridges
But that law grows weaker after every storm
The silence extends from the low to the ridges
And cancels your death grip and offers reform

I know that by now the strength pulses and weakens
And threatens to tumble under your weight
At last the light shines from the fires and the beacons
And you wake up to find that the feast is now bait.

Screaming hangover shakers
That will stalk out your brain
Will turn all that cool laughter
Into bright colored pain
The smell and the smoke plume
From the joint in your fist
Is chased by a shot and a beer
Into that white dragon mist
Then a round for the house
And I bet no one can tell
That nightmare difference
Between Heaven and Hell

The bartender's eyes are bleary
As he cries out "Last Call"
What a big drag this guy is
We just started this ball
Let's go on to your place
We can drink up the well
And start again tomorrow
Oh shit, you just fell
Say, can you hear that roll call
Between Heaven and Hell?

Between Heaven and Hell

Me and my friends were out
Drinking one day
When both God and the Devil
Told us to please go away
And said you don't want to drink here
And risk our wrath
For you've chosen the laughter
And the doper path
But if you do show up
And you dare ring that bell
You might find a surprise
Between Heaven and Hell

Now the blues band is blaring
Your favorite song
About that crimson jaded lady
That done you so wrong
You dance in your tears
As you try hard to yell
That she could tread that fine line
Between Heaven and Hell

There are friends right beside you
But also enemies near
One gives encouragement
The other tries fear
But you can tell their jive is slipping
That's why they live in a cell
And the Spirit in their séance is caught
Between Heaven and Hell

From a Barred Window

Diamonds shine on Queens of Shadow
Silver sparkles for the Master of the Day
Judges call what's fair and narrow
While their persecution puppets scream at bay

Down these streets
You'll see Sonny's sisters walking
Avenues that have no end
Well, they're beckoning to strangers stalking
Wares you cannot borrow or lend
An' so thin men carry leather
While night women fight for gold
And on the market place of no tomorrow
One is bought and one is sold
Now you pretend you've seen them coming
That you really knew from where
But when you reach out your good intentions
You will find there's no one there

And so diamonds shine on Queens of Shadow
An' silver sparkles for the Master of the Day
Those same judges call what's fair and narrow
While their persecution puppets scream at bay.

The Savage Song

And the tower winds down from famine
Returning to the souls that share deception
Even when the lies grow dimmer
And the masquerade is nearly over
Do the sign and scope of authors
Gain the turbulence of others
Like a Curse

Who are they to judge your slumbers
When your ancient soul surrendered
Are they pawns of the discretion
And faithful ownership of others
Steel and stones will bid you tidings
From the ovens of displeasure
While the bands encircle slowly
Vows of enmity and treasure
Like a Moan

Ocean windows by desertion
Prove the innocence of others
Yet they can still fill the distance
From between the heavens and your throne
But the promise shall be shattered
And your hovel be found empty
By the distant misty eye dreams
Of a Crone.

Curtains on Abandoned House

Veil—ghostly drifting through a
Pale afternoon—in silence
Your movements stir memories
Of terror unknown and long gone
        A reminder of life's once proud
Beauty—now the wreckage of old age
Still the skeleton of yesterday clings
To the form of today—a silent
Monument to patience.

Of Thieves,
Wizards
and Shards of Glass

Yes, thieves do bring to those who know
When Autumn buttons and children grow
The ring that slays the rhyme when fires dance slow
But you and I we shall always know
That everlasting nocturnal glow
And will approach with half drawn bow
And try to steal the common ring
That thieves do bring
While their temples burn
In healing snow.

Does not mingle with the pain
But the fortune teller told you
That tonight you'd be a cloud
Though it still feels
      Lonely in the Crowd

The night magician sits in the corner
Casting fish eyes at your show
With the stain of card receivers
And his helmet full of snow
With his pockets lined in whispers
That his victims scream out loud
Still the shivers in the shadows
Melt so
      Lonely in the Crowd

Above the clinking of the glasses
There's a rumor being spread
About the power of the dollar
While down the alley you're being led
And your unseen friend the merchant
Dishonors gestures that he vowed
And he winks behind his eyepatch
As he collects the
      Lonely in the Crowd

Then the ending comes in flashes
Lightning blades that stink of blood
The final thunder of dots and dashes
As they loosen away the flood
And on the sidewalk all the winos
And the whores stand with heads bowed
And silently look as if they are
      Lonely in the Crowd

Lonely in the Crowd
(Dime Note Blues)

I can hear the roar of laughter
That comes pouring out the door
And I'm standing by the lamppost
Then head in for what's in store
Well, the smoke smells like a shroud
And the music is way too loud
And I can see you're
      Lonely in the Crowd

The bad booze blends with the blues
And the bouncer looks so bored
So you take a chance with a smile and a dance
And hope it's one you can afford
Now there's a time for preservation
And a time you can be proud
And there's phony pleasures all around you
And you still
      Lonely in the Crowd

There's the ringing of the register
All the greed has turned to gold
Pay your dues to corner derbys
And glitter girls who turn to mold
For outside your trip is waiting
And the fog feels like a shroud
And you look as if you're
      Lonely in the Crowd

Now the ticket-selling jive studs
Clean their whistles in the rain
And you pray what you just paid for

Hasta la vida loca

Mr. Cool 30
To Maria 32
When the Legends Die 33
Castles in the Sky 34
Sorcerer's Moon 36
Kid Fang (Fourteen Measures of Time) 37
Scenario for Trumpets in June 38
Orphan Skyways 39
Blues for Moira 40
The Flower Cathedral 41
Love Song to a Geritol General
(or Prince Valiant Rides Again) 42
The Darkness Road 43
Of Coins 44
To Marie in Motion 45
Crosses: Alone 46
Epitaph 47
To Gods—Tin and Otherwise 48
Gallery Town (Tano's Bar) 49
Fortune Teller Baby (Sheila's Blues) 50
Visions of Michael Blind 51
Parables and Mirrors 52
A Dreamer's Question 53
Ode to the Cat (Oda al Gato) 54
The Merchant of Dreams 55
The Monkey Bite Blues
(Or the Captain Kept the Keys) 56
Thank u 58

Contents

On the Barbarian Dialects by Bill Whaley v

Richard Trujillo's "The Barbarian Dialects"
by John Nichols vii

For He Who Writes Below Radar
(Introductory comments for Richard's First Reading,
Café Tazza, Fall of 1999) by Rick Smith......................ix

Lonely in the Crowd (Dime Note Blues) 2

Of Thieves, Wizards and Shards of Glass.........................4

Curtains on Abandoned House..5

The Savage Song...6

From a Barred Window 7

Between Heaven and Hell 8

Mind Games No. 7..10

The Night of Two Assassins 11

Baby Load...12

Silver Strings (Epistle to an Enemy of Honor).................13

Reflections in a Dark Hour
(The Horseman) 14

Through These Halls of Anger 16

The Plague of Strangers 19

A Page of Hate
(Theme in Venom)..21

Fragments From a Siege 23

Requiem for a Vato Loco
(Death Watch: Part Three)...25

Tempest Lament in Blue 26

Images in the Morning Mist..28

Talons of Fate...29

others with fancier pedigrees he could have learned from, but could they rhyme with a back-beat?

A writer like Richard Trujillo flies below radar because sometimes we have the thing set pointed too high, to the heavens. Richard is right here among us, learning the lessons of life. He's here tonight—on our screen, ready to testify.

Ladies and Gentlemen, Richard Trujillo.

— Delivered by Rick Smith
7/16/99
Taos, New Mexico

For He Who Writes Below Radar
(Introductory comments for Richard's First Reading, Café Tazza, Summer of 1999)

USUALLY WHEN someone introduces a writer at one of these SOMOS readings, they give a list of schools, publications, workshops, etc. that the writer attended. Well, I can't do that for tonight's first reader because ... well, let's just say he flies below "literary radar."

Richard Trujillo is a native and life-long resident of Cañon. Between being born and being here, he's done a lot of things and spent a lot of time on the border—the border between the U.S. and Mexico, the border between life & death, the border between good & evil, between law & order ... the border between heaven and hell. Fortunately for all of us here tonight, Richard has ended up on the right side of the border. ·

I first heard about Richard Trujillo from Reuben at the post office, back when he worked the front window. Reuben and I would talk about all kinds of things. One day he mentioned this local guy named Richard who had lived this wild & crazy life and was writing a book about it. Reuben shrugged and said "Maybe he will"

Richard has done just that. His unpublished collection of poems is titled "The Barbarian Dialects" and it is everything a title like that promises. His poems bring forth all that he has collected in his heart and in his mind over the years. Some of it is loving and tender, some of it is painful and scary—all of it is real.

Richard's muse came to him via 50,000 watts of power over the open air, delivered by stations like KWKH from the mouths of men like Gatemouth, Chuck Berry and Little Richard. Later it was Dylan and Tom Waits, and scores of others through their vinyl likenesses. Of course, there are

All told the collection is a kind of ritual rock 'n roll poetry that exaggerates its every intention: think velvet painting meets Andy Warhol beside Ted Nugent's extravagant guitar and maybe Grand Theft Auto—none of it is all that removed from the gaudy sequence of violent video games. Richard Trujillo is a vato loco, his work is crude and full of those commonplace spasms that have addled the hoi polloi, once you accept the rules.

Richard Trujillo's "The Barbarian Dialects"
by John Nichols

THIS IS PRETTY RAW STUFF, not much artifice; academia or any other literary credentials gussy it up. Don't look for subtle. It's repetitive and melodramatic with zero apologies for the hardass drumbeats that propel it. The colorful clichés we all use in our stark moments keep coming at you like bullets from an assault rifle. The message and the meter come out of no formal education, and they teeter along on the edge of hysteria: angry, hyperbolic, simplistic, crazy (like a fox). Most of the rhythms are bluesy, and sometimes they like hip-hop and rap. They could be a combination of poetry, sci-fi metal music, or just a simple cry from the dark.

Nothing hypocritical or disingenuous here, most of it derives from a nasty funk shot through with a desire to be playful despite the chaotic world that Richard Trujillo lives in. There's a lot of laughter behind the sneering. These sardonic rhymes are downtown, inner city, though they were born in a rural ghetto. They come rocking and rolling along like Bobby Dylan, Kris Kristofferson played by Metallica, maybe Santana, possibly Public Enemy. Hard lives between the lines and nobody gets out alive.

This is askew and demented riffing, a collection of pop barbs and complaints. It sure ain't pretentious poetry. Mostly, it seems to me, these are just jive tunes and should all be set to music.

There's a lot of blood and doom straight from the headlines that daily surround us. "Why do your children die of drowning while my children die of thirst?" Good question. Go ask the "Captain with the Keys" or "Kid Fang," or "Mr. Cool" or the "Geritol General" himself. My favorites are "Baby Load," "The Monkey Bite Blues," "Kid Fang," "A Page of Hate," and "Lonely in the Crowd."

Bible a lot in jail or prison, because as he says, "That was the only book there."

One of the poet's most popular ballads is "Between Heaven and Hell" where "Screaming hangover shakers/that will stalk out your brain/Will turn all that cool laughter/Into bright colored pain."

The titles of "The Barbarian Dialects" reflect the experience of a man who has lived hard, loved, and seen the other side of life: "Thieves, Wizards, and Shards of Glass", "From a Barred Window," "Silver Strings" (Epistle to an Enemy of Honor), "Requiem for a Vato Loco," (Death Watch: Part Three), "Tempest Lament in Blue," "Mr. Cool," "To Maria," "Mirrors," "Ode to a Cat (Oda al Gato)."

The metaphors in his poetry reflect the concrete imagery of the street as well as the more abstract vocabulary of the passions elevated to metaphysical commentary. He possesses a kind of raw talent, nurtured by an existentialist's survival ethos. The lyrics are tinged with sarcasm and irony.

Richard and his neighbor, the santero Patrociño Barela, were friends. "We were in jail a couple of times at the same time when I was young," says Richard. "That guy kept us laughing all night. Man, he was great."

Richard's muse is nurtured by laughter, passion, and violence, producing an uncommon commentary on what it means to live the life of a Vato Loco. The language, like the life, is rich and expressive. The poetry dances to the beat of an unusually original singer.

On "The Barbarian Dialects"
by Bill Whaley

CAÑON'S POET, Richard Trujillo, a Chicano, born and bred, possesses the old-fashioned virtues of loyalty and authenticity in his life and in his art. Despite the demons found in Richard's demi-monde, he survives, which is what his lyrics are all about.

When Richard was a young man, he was volatile, quick-tempered. "Now," he says, "I just walk away from these fools. I'm too old for that stuff. A lot of my friends are dead from needles. I used to know a lot of bad-ass gangsters. Manners and respect kept me alive. I dropped out of school in the tenth grade. I was in the guard from '57 to '59. I was in prison in '61-'62, for 18 months, for breaking and entering.

"The Sheriff, Fasho Trujillo, drove me and a friend down. Stopped in Española and bought us a beer. When we got to the joint, the guards gave Fasho hell for not having us in shackles. He said, 'know these boys. They're friends of mine.' He was good people. After I got paroled, I did not go back, not in 37 years."

"The Barbarian Dialects," Richard's first volume of poetry, was much influenced by listening to the blues. He grew up hanging out with older guys, listening to Chuck Berry, Ray Charles, James Brown, among other black artists. Later he listened to Bob Dylan and Tom Waits.

Sudden violence is never far from Richard's verse. For instance in the poem "Lonely in the Crowd," the poet writes, "Then the ending comes in flashes/Lightning blades that stink of blood/The final thunder of dots and dashes/As they loosen away the flood ..."

Though his friends have given him a lot of books, he says "I don't know where it (poetry) comes from sometimes." Richard has no formal education but he read the

The Barbarian Dialects
© Copyright 1997 Richard Trujillo. All Rights Reserved.

Author: Richard Trujillo
On the Barbarian Dialects: Bill Whaley
Richard Trujillo's "The Barbarian Dialects": by John Nichols
For He Who Writes Below Radar: by Rick Smith
Editor: Bill Whaley
Copy Editing / Proofing by Helen Rynaski and Steve Fox
Graphic Design: WinkVisual Arts
Cover Photo by Maria

FIRST EDITION 2017

ISBN: 978-0-9973950-1-3

the Barbarian Dialects

by

Richard Trujillo

the Barbarian Dialects

www.ingramcontent.com/pod-product-compliance
Lightning Source LLC
Chambersburg PA
CBHW030449010526
4418CB000118/857